DATE DUE

NEW AT THE ZOO

NEW AT THE ZOO

Animal Offspring From Aardvark To Zebra

By TERRY SHANNON
and CHARLES PAYZANT

Illustrated with photographs

GOLDEN GATE JUNIOR BOOKS
SAN CARLOS, CALIFORNIA

For Margaret and Hugh

FOREWORD

A man is ethical only when life, as such, is sacred to him, that of plants and animals as that of his fellow-man, and when he devotes himself helpfully to all life that is in need of help.

Albert Schweitzer *(Out Of My Life And Thought)*

Early association with animals is a means of providing valuable experience and of establishing a respect for all life. As a boy, when a farm dog or barn cat gave birth to offspring I would search for the hidden nest until I found the living treasure within. Smelling the milk odor of the litter and feeling the softness and warmth of the baby animals against my hands and face was sheer joy. When unwanted puppies and kittens met a harsh death at the hands of a budget-conscious farmer, my heart, along with that of the deprived mother dog or cat, was broken as I watched her brief but aimless search for the lost offspring. To this day, thought of that scene gives me sobering pause. It has, I feel, gentled my hands in work with animals.

Not every youth has the advantage of such association with nature's creatures. Many children do not have the opportunity to marvel at the ways of animals and their young while visiting or living on a farm; they are unable to observe animal mother-craft at first-hand. Communities dedicated solely to commerce and industry do not provide for learning experiences of this kind. How then can mature concern for wildlife and nature be engendered? How can today's youth secure those humanizing qualities taught by association with animals?

New At The Zoo is a book that describes how many communities are accomplishing this. It tells how children across the land, from areas near New York's Bronx Zoo to those of the Greater Los Angeles Zoo in California, are imbued with the feeling that the animals within such parks are theirs. Now, through zoo visits, hundreds of school children can follow the progressing pregnancies and births of some of the world's most interesting animals. We know by experience and from voluminous correspondence from children that they relate to these events on a strong personal basis. Children who may never hope to see a mare foal in a rural farm setting may possibly witness the birth of a camel calf in the Los Angeles Zoo, the arrival of a baby giraffe in the Zoo at San Diego, or other similar events in other zoos throughout North America.

Children who may never hope to see a bobcat with its cubs in the wild may experience the dramatic sight of zoo-born lion cubs with their mother as she brings them from their den for the first time. Many young zoo visitors, unable to look into a meadow-lark's nest in the fields, can see for themselves the miracle of a baby chick pecking its way out of the egg.

New At The Zoo is about experiences such as these. The authors have told in charming style authentic accounts of animal offspring who live in our zoos and animal parks; they have focused their cameras well and have been "there" when it counted.

CHARLES J. SEDGWICK, D.V.M.
Resident Veterinarian,
San Diego Zoo

San Diego, California
May, 1972

ACKNOWLEDGMENTS

To Dr. Charles Sedgwick of the San Diego Zoo, a sensitive, dedicated man with a deep reverence for all life, who has alleviated the sufferings of many of nature's creatures, we offer warm thanks and appreciation for writing the Foreword for this book. And for their generous cooperation in furnishing special information, photographs, or other special services, our appreciation and thanks go to the following governmental agencies and representatives, zoos and wild animal parks, together with those of their personnel who were especially helpful:

Australian Consul-General, the Hon. Philip R. Searcy; John C. Hanafin, Consul (Information)

Cincinnati Zoo, Edward J. Maruska, Director; Pepper Wilson

Le Jardin des Merveilles, Jardin Zoologique, Montreal, Raymond Roth, Assistant Superintendent

Lincoln Park Zoological Gardens, Chicago, Dr. Lester E. Fisher, Director; Mark A. Rosenthal, Associate Curator of Mammals

Lion Country Safari, Harry Shuster, President; Jerry Kobrin, Vice President; Walter C. (Pat) Quinn III, Zoological Director (California); John Foxson

National Zoological Park (Smithsonian Institution), Dr. Theodore H. Reed, Director; Sybil (Billie) Hamlet

New York Zoological Park (The Bronx Zoo), William G. Conway, Director; Edward R. Ricciuti

Oklahoma City Zoo, Lawrence Curtis, Director; Patricia Manville

San Diego Zoological Park (and San Diego Wild Animal Park), Dr. Charles Schroeder, Director; William J. Seaton; JoAnn Thomas; Carole Towne

Storyland Valley Zoo, Edmonton, D. J. Hudson, Supervisor

United States Fish and Wildlife Service, Bureau of Sport Fisheries and Wildlife (Dept. of the Interior, the Hon. Rogers Morton, Secretary); Beatrice Boone

Zoological Society of London (Regent's Park Zoo), Professor Sir Solly Zuckerman, Secretary; Michael Lyster

Dianne Capachin of the Walter D. Stone Memorial Zoo, Stoneham, Mass.

And our thanks to all the delightful animal offspring and their parents pictured in this book for allowing us to be their friends and share them with our readers.

Whether it be a spindly-legged, long-necked giraffe, a tawny lion, or a rare black-footed ferret, creatures of the wild are a never-ending source of interest and wonder. Whether striped tiger, intricately-patterned snake, or well-feathered eagle, each of nature's beings commands our fascinated attention.

Whatever their habitat in the wild, whatever their life-style, however widely they may differ in size and appearance, creatures of the earth share one thing in common—they procreate. They reproduce and have offspring, each after its own kind. The ingenious ways in which wild creatures care for their young is part of the miracle of nature.

In this age of city living few of us have the privilege of seeing the wondrous creatures of nature in the wild state. Not for us the pleasure of peeking into the nurseries of the wild kingdom to see animal babies in den, lair, burrow, or nest.

Modern zoos, however, make it possible to have a close-up look at infant animals in varying stages of growth, cared for by animal parents or by substitute human "parents." Whole family groups of wildlife, including newly-born offspring, are sometimes to be seen together at the zoo.

Baby Okapi gets a gentle face-washing with mother's big tongue.

Of particular interest to most people are the mammals, those creatures who are born live and are nursed by the mother. Among these are the familiar lions, tigers, elephants, and bears. There are dozens of others not so familiar, such as the richly-colored okapi which is closely related to the giraffe.

For some people, in spite of possible feelings of apprehension or even revulsion, there is nothing to hold the interest like a reptile, be it alligator, lizard, or snake.

Downy baby birds, the young of waterfowl such as ducks, swans, cranes, and a host of others, have universal appeal.

10

Attention of one Snow Leopard cub is drawn elsewhere as its twin playfully attacks mother in their Oklahoma City Zoo home.

Some scientists believe that the day may come when the only remnants of wildlife left on earth will be those cared for in zoos.

Hundreds of kinds of wild creatures have already vanished from the earth within past decades, their living forms never to be seen again. There are hundreds more threatened with a similar fate. The snow leopard, the American alligator, and the bald eagle are but a few of those for whom time is running out.

Young American Bald Eagles (left) in nest on offshore pinnacle of an Aleutian island. Heads will turn white at maturity like these (below) in rookery of Bird of Prey Aviary, San Diego Zoo, on loan from the United States Fish and Wildlife Service for scientific, educational and exhibition purposes. The Bald Eagle is the national symbol of the United States.

Six-hour-old nestling Sandhill Crane at Malheur Refuge, Burns, Oregon. Chicks of this species are sometimes mistaken for Whooping Crane chicks.

Zoos and governmental agencies trying to halt the loss of wildlife sometimes work together. In an effort to save the nearly extinct whooping crane, eggs that otherwise might not have hatched were carefully taken from the wild and artificially incubated. As a result, a dozen or so healthy chicks have been raised to maturity at the Patuxent Wildlife Center at Laurel, Maryland. Other whooping cranes are being cared for in the Audubon Park Zoo in New Orleans, Louisiana, and in the San Antonio Zoo in Texas. Eaglets too have been hatched from eggs at Patuxent. And there are eagles in enormous aviaries in the Cincinnati and San Diego Zoos, among others, where they have room to spread their wings and take off in soaring flight.

This twenty-eight-day-old Whooping Crane is one of five chicks hatched as a result of an experiment carried on jointly by the Canadian Wildlife Service and the United States Bureau of Sport Fisheries and Wildlife. Chicks were cared for at the Patuxent Wildlife Center, a research station of the U. S. Department of Interior, Bureau of Sport Fisheries and Wildlife.

12

Rare Scimitar-horned Oryx mother and baby are at home in the San Diego Zoo.

Zoos and animal parks have undertaken selective breeding projects, hopeful that rare and endangered creatures will mate and reproduce in captivity. Special attention is given to the care and preservation of resultant offspring so that they will have a chance to grow to maturity and themselves reproduce. It is because of these efforts that we are able now to see certain of the threatened species and their young. The graceful scimitar-horned oryx, for example, has been successfully bred in captivity and infant oryx are thriving in zoological gardens and animal parks. Many species of African wildlife, in addition to the oryx, are threatened with extinction through reduced territories and because of illegal hunting. The sad story is that as human populations spread out in expanding countries, animal populations are crowded out or hunted to extinction.

Bison (Buffalo) cows and calves at Wichita Wildlife Refuge, Oklahoma.

The American bison, or buffalo, as it is often called, is an example of a threatened species snatched back from the edge of oblivion. In the 1800's great herds of bison thundered across the land. The coming of civilization and the popularity of buffalo robes almost exterminated these creatures of the plains. Organized hunting parties killed millions of them. More often than not, only the hide was taken, and perhaps the tongue, which was considered a delicacy. The rest of the carcass was left to rot.

In the early 1900's when there were few bison left in the wild, the New York Zoological Park (the Bronx Zoo) had four bulls and three cows. Within a few years this small herd had produced a fine crop of bawling offspring. The Zoo then offered the United States Government the start of a bison herd and the animals selected were placed in the Wichita Forest Reserve in Oklahoma. Descendants of that original herd may be seen today in various zoos throughout the world.

Today in the wild, polar bears are relentlessly shot down by trophy hunters. Their numbers are decreasing rapidly, with fewer and fewer cubs to carry on the species. Fortunate is the zoo which is able to rear the furry white creatures. Everyone, it seems, enjoys watching these natives of the bleak, icy arctic regions. Surprisingly, polar bears take well to captivity and to the heat of summer.

Zoo-born cubs are kept in the darkness of the maternity den for about four months before the mother allows them to venture further. A mother polar bear is among the most devoted of animal parents. In the privacy of the den she nurses the cubs and grooms them until they are frisky young toddlers. When Frieda Polar Bear of the San Diego Zoo finally allowed her twins* to emerge into the outdoor exhibit area, one promptly fell into the pool, much to its own surprise. Frieda hurriedly pulled it out by the scruff of the neck. Even though the cub appeared to swim well, a walk around the pool was apparently all that Frieda had planned for that day's outing.

*Named Castor and Pollux for the twin stars in the constellation Gemini.

The Golden Marmoset, a New World monkey, has been all but squeezed out of its natural habitat in Brazil. This little primate now lives in an area so small that its chances for survival are remote. The males take care of the babies, efficiently overseeing their behavior, training them in marmoset ways. Father gives them back to mother only at feeding time. Babies usually ride on father's back as he scampers about through the tree branches high in the Brazilian forests. Seldom more than nine inches long, the little creatures have bright reddish fur and a lion-like mane.

The San Diego Zoo in Balboa Park is among those designated* as one of the depots for the reproduction of the Golden Marmoset. There is a scientific staff doing field work in Brazil, studying this animal's nutrition, its diseases and its parasites. Every effort is being made to have the marmosets reproduce in their native territory as well as in captivity. The aim in captive breeding is to get beyond the first, second, third and fourth generations and maintain established breeding colonies. Since both sexes share in the care and feeding of the young, if one parent fails, the baby dies. The San Diego Zoo has done well with its breeding of these animals that are so rare, both in the wild and in captivity.

This Zoo has been remarkably successful in the breeding and rearing of many other species as well, the orangutan among them, as we shall see later. Once there was a large population of orangutans in the wild but forests of Southeast Asia in which they lived were cut down, greatly reducing their living areas. Now they are found in the wild only on the Islands of Borneo and Sumatra, their numbers reduced to a few thousand.

These creatures are protected by Indonesian law but many are taken illegally. No responsible zoo, however, will accept illegally taken orangs, or any other illegally taken animal. Thus the orang breeding program is of the utmost importance.

To breed well in captivity animals must feel comfortable in their surroundings, with sufficient privacy when they wish to hide from zoo visitors or others of their own kind. Diet must be suitable to their needs, and sufficiently like that enjoyed in the wild, to satisfy them.

*By the Conservation Committee of the American Association of Zoological Parks and Aquariums.

Golden Marmoset Family

The strange Proboscis Monkey, one of the Old World monkeys, is difficult to maintain in captivity. Named for its big nose, it is a native of Borneo. The male of the species makes a honking noise through its great proboscis, which continues to grow as long as he lives. The first baby Proboscis Monkey to be born outside Indonesia was born at the San Diego Zoo. The young

monkeys are very active. Fun for them is tweaking their parents' noses or swinging on their tails. When parents tire of this they send the children packing.

One of the difficulties in maintaining these unusual creatures is their preference for a diet of leaves, shoots, and buds of such plants as cup-of-gold, hibiscus, and eugenia. All of these grow in profusion in southern regions of California.

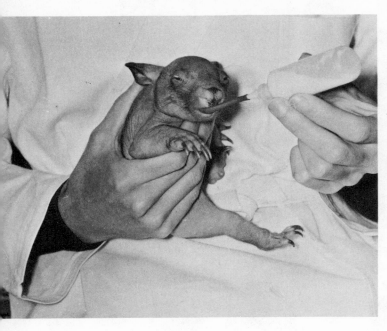

This baby Hairy-nosed Wombat being cared for by a human "mother" will be fully furred by the time it is about six months old. In the wild it would live in the mother's pouch until that time. The wombat lives in burrows which it scoops out with its shovel-like claws (below).

Official agencies of many countries have been slow to realize the need to save creatures native to them. Others have begun to take positive steps to do so. Australia is one of the leaders in this regard. Both the Australian government and the zoos of that country are very conscious of the need to preserve their wildlife heritage.

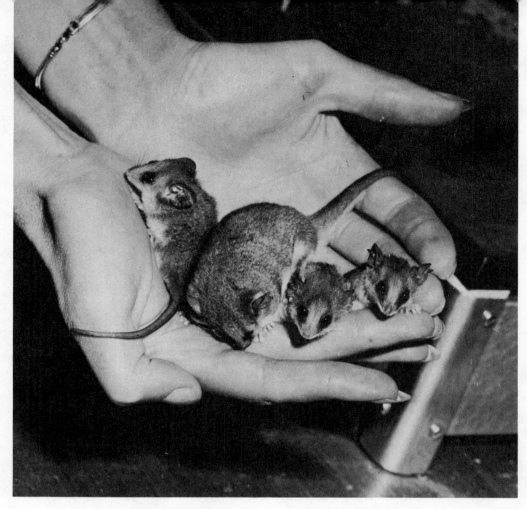

Female Pigmy Possum and her three babies which she carried in her tiny pouch until they grew their own fur coats. This small marsupial species can rear no more than four young at a time.

Australian zoos have had considerable success in the breeding in captivity of many creatures native to their continent. Surplus animals are quite frequently offered to the zoos of other countries. Among the wildlife of Australia are certain species not found elsewhere. This is believed to be due to the continent's isolation from the rest of the world since prehistoric times, geologic ages ago.

Nearly half of Australia's native mammals are marsupials— animals which produce their young in an undeveloped state and rear them in a pouch.

Nine-month-old Great Grey Kangaroo joey has become quite a pocketful and is nearly ready to leave mother's pouch permanently. Meantime, the discomfort of having a large and still-growing hind foot poking out beside one's ear is a small price to pay for the warmth and security of the pouch.

Kangaroos, on exhibit in many zoos, are perhaps the best known of these Australian natives. They vary in size from the tiny rat-kangaroo which is about eighteen inches from nose to tail tip, to the great grey kangaroo which is more than seven feet tall when it stands erect.

Joey, as all kangaroo babies are called, is only a couple of inches long at birth.* Underdeveloped, blind and without fur, it finds its way up into the mother's pouch. There it stays until it is fully furred and no longer fits into the carrying case that has been its home for four or more months. By the time the young kangaroo is ousted from it, to be on its own, the pouch is stretched to capacity, nearly dragging on the ground from joey's weight. If frightened while becoming adjusted to life outside, a joey will still try to dive headfirst back into the safety of the pouch.

*This varies from a fraction of an inch to two inches or so, depending on the species.

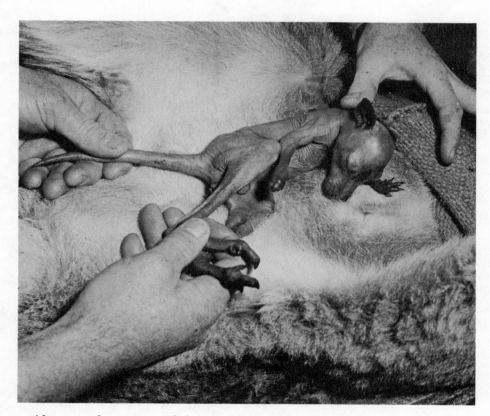

About to be measured by members of an Australian scientific research team, this little joey was soon snug in his mother's pouch again. Now just over four months old, it was about 3/4" long at birth.

Mother feeds on gum (eucalyptus) leaves as Snowy, the rare white Koala at the Taronga Park Zoo, Sydney, holds tight to her. Mother's head is somewhat camouflaged by tree bark.

The appealing koala is on exhibit outside its native Australia only at the San Diego Zoo. This cuddly-looking creature's diet consists solely of eucalyptus leaves, of which there is an abundance in the botanical gardens of this Southern California zoo. In these homelike surroundings the koalas have mated successfully and baby koalas have been a welcome addition to the Zoo's extensive attractions.

Like the kangaroo, the mother koala carries her baby in a pouch when it is young. As it grows older, mother sometimes carries baby on her back or holds it in her arms. When frightened, the baby koala cries like a human baby. These lovable, teddy-bear-like animals sleep during most of the day and feed at night. The tree-dwelling koala* is rarely known to drink, apparently getting sufficient moisture from the leaves they eat.

*An aboriginal word meaning "no drink."

24

Adult Kookaburras with two young, plus clutch of eggs at the base of a stump, in the National Zoological Park, Washington, D. C. This Zoo has an outstanding record for breeding these odd birds in captivity. Largest of the world's kingfishers, this bird may never eat a single fish in its life, its diet consisting of such things as small snakes, lizards, crabs, and mice. The kookaburra's rollicking laughter is part of the various calls and sounds it has evolved.

Among birds native to Australia is the kookaburra (laughing jackass) and the flightless emu, second only in size to the ostrich. Among native reptiles is the tiger snake. Though relatively small, this snake is one of the most poisonous in the world. Whereas most snakes lay eggs, the tiger snake gives birth to live offspring.

Tiger Snake behind protective glass, San Diego Zoo.

Australian Squirrel Glider.

This Pigmy Glider mother, though not as big as a mouse, here carries her baby on her back. Rarely more than 5½″ long, this dainty creature is the midget of the possum family.

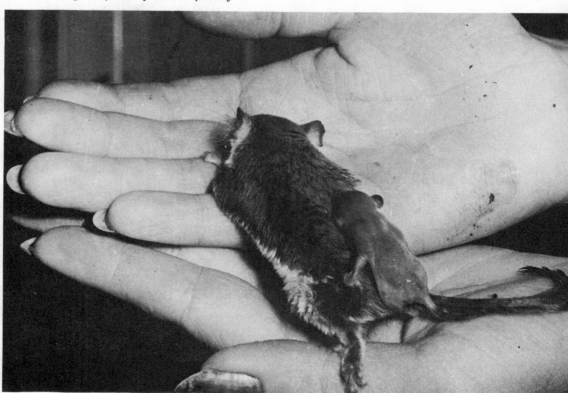

The most unusual native creatures of Australia are the echidna (or spiny ant-eater), and the platypus. They are among the greatest animal oddities in the world and the only surviving members of the Monotremes, or egg-laying mammals. The female echidna develops a pouch only during the breeding season, into which she deposits one soft-shelled egg. After hatching, the embryo young is suckled in the pouch until it is somewhat more developed. It is then cast out and hidden in a hole in the ground where the mother feeds it with milk at irregular intervals.

(above) An Echidna, or Spiny Ant-eater, at the Wildlife Sanctuary at Healesville, Australia, searches for insects with its long tubular snout. Its spines do not develop until after it is cast out of the mother's pouch. If it feels threatened with danger (opposite), the echidna rolls itself into a prickly ball.

28

Platypus nest and eggs. An Australian halfpenny, which is one inch in diameter, is shown beside the eggs; a fifteen-inch ruler lies in front of the nest.

The platypus is sometimes described as a living link with mammals, birds, and reptiles. It has a furry coat, a beaver-like tail, webbed feet, and a broad, leathery, duck-like bill. The female lays one, two, or three eggs at breeding time, but the usual number is two. She then curls her body around them, serving as an incubator for about ten to fourteen days. The shell of a platypus egg is similar to that of most reptile eggs, of a parchment-like texture so that it cannot crack.

On hatching, the embryo-like infant has no trace of the duckbill. It obtains milk by nuzzling the mother's abdomen. This causes milk to flow from a milk duct and the baby sucks it up from the mother's fur. The platypus does not have nipple-equipped breasts as do other mammals. After many weeks, showing short little bills, the young platypuses emerge from the burrow to follow their mother about and to play and swim in the water.

The platypus inhabits rivers, lakes, creeks, and small water holes. Two burrows are constructed along the banks of these waterways, one in which the male and female live and another to which the female retires to lay her eggs.

A well-grown Platypus, startled by camera lights, pauses in its journey through the water.

Male Platypus showing sharp hind claw which secretes a poison, its sole means of defense.

Platypuses brought from the wild are kept in Australian zoos hopeful of establishing a breeding program. The platypus was bred in captivity for the first and only time, so far, at the Healesville Wildlife Sanctuary, near Melbourne, in 1945. In late 1971 two eggs were discovered at the Taronga Zoo in Sydney, but hopes for their hatching were dashed when a few weeks later they were found to be shriveled and dead. Zoologists are continually striving to learn more and more of the ways and needs of this unusual creature.

Although they did not breed, a pair of platypuses lived for ten years in the Bronx Zoo, seemingly content in their water tank and river-bank-like burrow.

It is the dream of many a zoo man to have a pair of breeding platypuses who will raise their young to maturity. For it is the dream of concerned men that rare creatures of such interest as these shall not vanish from the earth.

Platypus in glass-sided tank at the Healesville Sanctuary. It was here that the platypus was bred for the first time in captivity in 1945. The platypus, an air-breathing, aquatic animal, averages about two feet in length.

Scientists at various zoos and research centers are trying to find answers to many questions about our fellow creatures by studying animal children and their parents. Why do animals do what they do? How do certain animals communicate with one another? What are their diseases and how best to cure them? What are ideal breeding conditions and how do they vary from one species to another?

Zoologists believe that if they come to have a better understanding of the ways of mammals, birds, and reptiles, as well as their diseases, they will be able to save many of the endangered species.

Those who foster animal breeding programs are beginning to realize that all animals do not necessarily live by instinct alone. Some must learn certain behavior patterns from their parents and others of their kind. This is one of the problems encountered in raising first-generation young creatures within the confines of a zoo.

Before the days of zoo nurseries and children's zoos where some young animals are cared for, zoo keepers' wives as well as keepers themselves became substitute mothers for many infant zoo-born or orphaned wild-caught creatures. Apartments and houses, whether large or small, were apt to be overrun with tiny lion cubs, young monkeys, or any one of dozens of kinds of animal offspring. Even today, many animal babies are saved through home care until they can safely be placed back in zoo quarters.

It was in the mid-1940's that the nursery at the New York Zoological Park was established, thought to be the first anywhere. A converted storeroom in the Lion House was decorated to look as much like a human baby nursery as possible. When ready for occupancy it had a pale-pink ceiling, with baby-blue walls on which hung pictures of young animals.

Three zoo-born tiger cubs were the first occupants. They were four months old, fat and thriving after being cared for at home by a zookeeper's wife from the time of their birth. There followed a variety of young creatures which included, at one time or another, everything from a leopard to a tiny deer.

Devoted people responsible for newly-born animals take every precaution to see that they survive. An example of this was vividly demonstrated at the Lion Country Safari animal park in

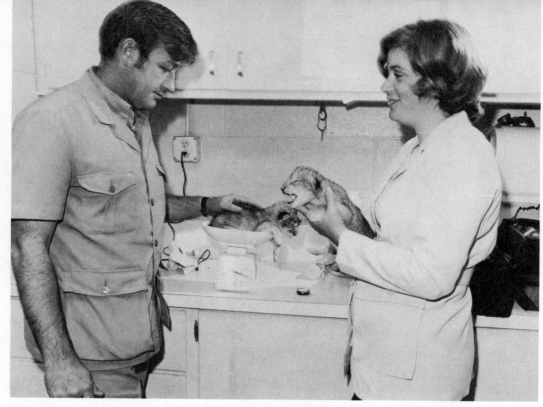

Walter C. (Pat) Quinn III, Lion Country Safari Zoological Director, and Beth Campbell weigh infant Lion cubs.

Laguna Hills, California, when a lioness was unable to care for her cubs at the time of birth. One of the litter of three was born dead, a mere spark of life in the other two. The Zoological Director and a nursery attendant applied mouth-to-mouth resuscitation for fifteen minutes before the infant cubs began to breathe on their own. Each of the babies received needed medication at the hands of the Park's veterinarian. Cared for then in the nursery, they lived to grow into lively, playful young cubs.

The human "mothers" in zoo nurseries are usually girls, many of whom have been zoology or biology students, or with some experience in the care of animals. The girls prepare the food for their young charges, feed them, play with them, and record their progress.

At Lion Country Safari the girls who work in the nursery and the Junior Jungle may hand-feed as many as forty babies three times a day. These may include, at varying times, a litter of opossum, baby hippopotamuses, young elephants, monkeys, little llamas, and any number of bleating young goats.

Three times a day tubs filled with apples, bananas, lettuce, and meat are brought into the large nursery kitchen. One of the attendants slices up the fruit, another prepares the meat, while yet another girl heats the special milk formulas. Milk mixtures for the babies are specially fortified with vitamins.

A baby elephant may drink three half-gallon containers of milk, or even more, at each feeding. A baby fox devours a portion of raw meat, while a six-month-old Malaysian sun bear lives on a diet of apples, bananas, bread and honey.

Baby lions are perhaps the most difficult of the animal children to feed. Once they are trained to drink from a bottle they are reluctant to release the source of their food and struggle with sharp little claws to keep the bottle, even when it is empty. As infant lions grow into gangling, playful youngsters they rough and tumble with each other and are quick to pounce on any human who comes near.

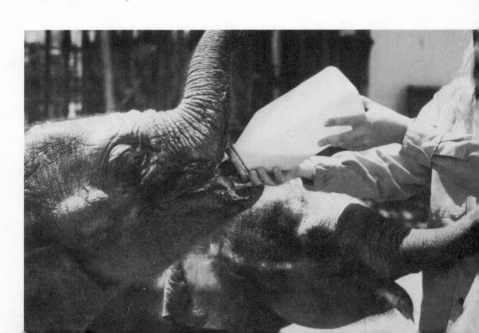

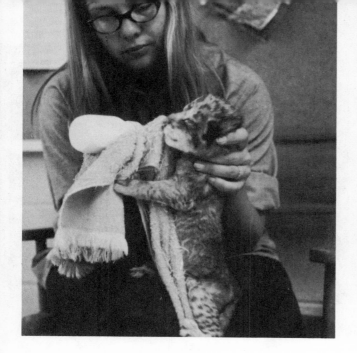

Playful Lion cub has designs on author-photographer Terry Shannon's camera.

After being weaned, the young are cared for until they are old enough to take care of themselves with others of their kind out on the large preserve. Age of maturity to this stage varies among different kinds of animals. A lion cub may be introduced into the pride after about a year. An elephant may be three or four years of age or older before it is ready to leave the baby animal compound and take its place with its elders.

Elephants are difficult to breed in captivity because of the killer instincts of the bull elephant at mating time, even though he may be reasonably gentle at other times. The first elephant baby to be born in a zoological garden in this country was at the Washington Park Zoo in Portland, Oregon. Within half an hour of its birth, with a helpful nudge from mama, a two- or three-hundred-pound elephant baby may be standing on shaky little legs, contentedly nursing. In the wild, a mother elephant may have help caring for her baby from other females in the herd.

Marcie Wallaby peeks across at Margo from the terry-cloth pouch that serves as a substitute for her mother's furry one.

Margo, baby Pig-tailed Macaque, contentedly sucks her thumb in her glass-sided playpen at the San Diego Zoo nursery.

Today most of the larger, modernized zoos have nurseries or special rooms in which zoo-born infant animals or young wild-caught ones can be cared for.

The facility at the San Diego Zoo is an outstanding example of a modern zoo nursery. It was there that Juba, the only baby cheetah born in the United States to survive more than a few days, was cared for.* The cheetah is another creature of the wild for whom time is running out. Every effort is being made to save it from extinction.

Juba was born at the San Diego Wild Animal Park near Escondido, a branch of the San Diego Zoo. His mother was in a group being studied by a research team in charge of a cheetah breeding project. Juba was one of a litter of three. Unfortunately, two of the cubs were killed by adult cheetahs in the enclosure before they could be rescued. The surviving cub was hurried off to the nursery in Balboa Park where he was given every care in a desperate attempt to keep him alive. At first, the tiny cub was fed two teaspoons of a fortified formula for babies every two hours.

*Subsequently a cheetah at the Toledo (Ohio) Zoo produced a litter of four cubs. And on April 28, 1972, Juba's mother gave birth to another litter of three. The cubs were left with the mother at the Park since she was taking good care of them, nursing them and moving them in the heat of the day from bright sunlight to the shade of a bush.

As Juba grew and became more sturdy the time between feedings was lengthened. Quantities were gradually increased until he was drinking milk from a bottle and eating small amounts of cat food. Little Juba made birdlike sounds when calling for food, or if he became alarmed.

Visitors crowded around to watch through the nursery windows as the rare and beautiful cub was fed. They looked on with delight as he scampered around the room or slept in his playpen. This small member of the big cat family enjoyed tussling with his toy lion, but was quick to hiss if he felt threatened. When he was born Juba weighed nineteen ounces. At three months he weighed over twelve pounds. A fully-grown cheetah weighs from about ninety to 125 pounds.

When he was about four months old the lanky young cub joined others of his kind back where he was born in the Park located in the San Pasqual Valley. There, in comparative freedom, he roams about or stretches his long legs to run over the hills, or lies dozing in the warm sun. It is hoped that he will father a long line of cheetah cubs who will help to maintain the species generation after generation. Cubs are born with the distinctive black tear lines which are characteristic of these animals.

Maggie and Bob Orangutan.

Shortly before Juba left the nursery a tiny orangutan, Ken-Alan, was born at the Zoo to Maggie and Bob Orangutan. Maggie, also zoo-born, knew little about being a mother and in her case instinct alone was not enough. In the wild, young apes observe the older ones in all the affairs of living. They watch their elders mate, bear offspring, and care for them. The young learn from the older ones. In captivity Maggie had not had this opportunity to learn all the ways of orangutans.

When Ken-Alan was born Maggie held him by one little leg and pulled him around like a toy, making no attempt to nurse him. In shock and blue with cold, the infant was rescued by zoo personnel. He was given medical attention, swaddled in baby blankets, and fed from a tiny nursing bottle. Then, warm and cozy, he was placed in an incubator where he stayed for several weeks. A pacifier was as comforting to Ken-Alan as it is to human babies.

Sue Schroeder, nursery attendant, reaches in to tuck blankets securely around the tiny Ken-Alan.

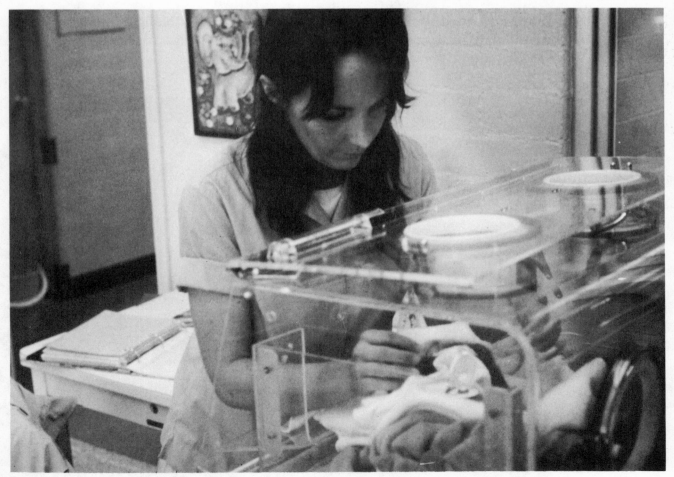

Now six months old, Ken-Alan (called Boom Orang on some of his many TV appearances), nibbles his human mother's thumb as she rocks him before putting him to bed.

This infant orang developed into a sturdy baby who liked to play with toys, enjoyed his warm bath, and took his food with gusto. The loving care showered on him by his surrogate mother was a special ingredient in the formula on which he grew into a bouncing, good-natured youngster. Like human babies, other mammal offspring respond to love and discipline. And, like human babies, they have distinct personalities.

A big smile and a hug for "mama," JoAnn Thomas.

It's serious business trying to catch a drink while getting a bath.

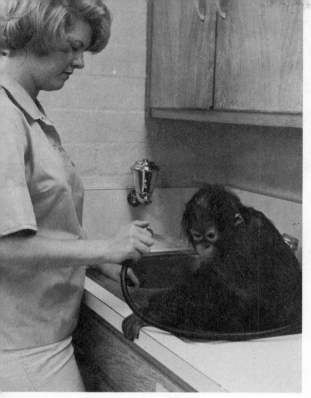

All rinsed off, ready for a big fluffy towel.

Where's my mama gone?

Hair all dry and fluffy, Ken-Alan reaches both arms up to find it really is squeaky clean.

*A year-old Ken-Alan goes explor-
ing, all dressed up in his new suit.*

When Ken-Alan was six months old a little half-sister named
Karen came to share the nursery with him. Born of different
mothers, they had the same father.

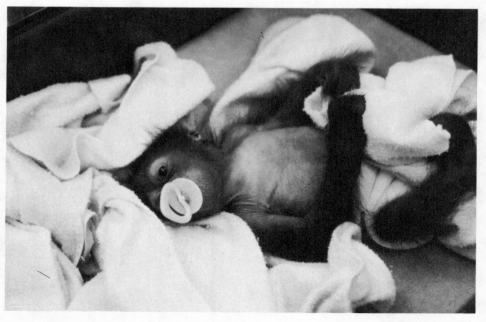

A pacifier is a big comfort to baby Karen.

Three-months-old Karen hugs her big toy rabbit while dropping off to sleep.

Time to wake up?

At six months Karen still enjoys her bottle, and dearly loves Jo-Ann, the "mother" she shares with Ken-Alan.

Carol Elephant celebrates a birthday with the help of young friends. Pigmy Chimps Lorel and Linette are held by JoAnn Thomas and Polly Lewis. Linette was the first Pigmy Chimpanzee born in the U. S.

Birthdays are fun! It doesn't worry Ken-Alan that the bakery put an extra "l" in his name as he gets to work on one of the intriguing packages waiting for him.

44

Many human children have private parties in today's zoos, a wonderful way to celebrate a birthday, with all the guests visiting the animals. Zoo animal children, too, sometimes have birthday parties.

When Ken-Alan was a year old his foster mother had a party for him. It was complete with a cake with one big candle, presents, and party hats. Baby Karen, a large rabbit from the Children's Zoo, and a visiting timber wolf named Sylvester were among the guests at the party.

(above) It's "Let the party begin" as Ken-Alan seems to be telling Karen she'd better take the pacifier out of her mouth if she expects to taste his yummy cake. (opposite) Party over, Sylvester says a polite "thank you for a nice time" and bids goodbye to a tired Birthday Boy and a sleeping Karen, safe in the arms of Kirstie Shaw.

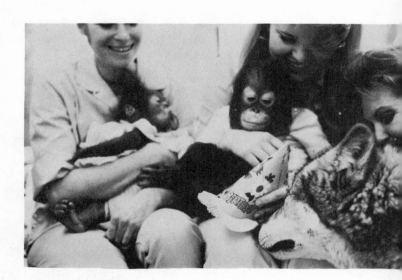

Zoos sometimes send their animals visiting in order to assemble a pair for the purpose of mating. Perhaps the best known instance of this was with the only two giant pandas outside of China at that time. Chi Chi, a female panda owned by London's Regent's Park Zoo, and the Moscow Zoo's male panda, An An, exchanged visits several times. But on none of these occasions would Chi Chi have anything to do with An An. She eluded his every attempt at mating. It was a disappointment to panda lovers the world over that no baby pandas came to bless either zoo.

Su-Lin, the first panda ever to leave China, was brought to the United States as a baby in 1936. He went to live in Chicago's Brookfield Zoo where he enchanted visitors by turning somersaults, and with other childlike activities. During the following five years two other pandas joined Su-Lin in Chicago; four went to the Bronx Zoo and two to the St. Louis Zoo. It was a sad day when the last of these pandas died, for they could not then be replaced.

In 1972 giant pandas once more came to America. A celebrated young pair, Ling-Ling, a female, and Hsing-Hsing, a male, arrived at the National Zoo in Washington, D. C., a gift of the People's Republic of China. Hopes were sent soaring that at maturity the two would mate and a baby panda would be born at the Zoo.

Extremely rare, the endearing panda is native only to a small region high in the rugged mountains of Tibet and China. In captivity no animal is more appealing in looks or more amusing in its play than the roly-poly panda.

Chi Chi (foreground) runs from An An in London's Regent's Park Zoo.

46

Ling-Ling makes herself right at home in her new quarters at the National Zoo as she reaches for a tasty morsel of bamboo.

The Chinese have successfully bred the giant panda in captivity. The first such birth was in the Peking Zoo in 1963. A baby panda may weigh no more than a few ounces at birth and grow to be six feet tall, weighing 300 pounds or more. The Chinese are making a study of the pandas in their zoos, carefully recording their habits, food requirements, and mating times.

Continued life in the wild for a remote neighbor of the giant panda, the Douc Langur, is doubtful. This langur is one of four endangered species of Old World monkeys native to Southern Asia. It is an inhabitant of the war-torn jungles of Vietnam, Laos, and Cambodia. Like many monkey species, langurs live in family groups, baby clinging to mother until it is able to fend for itself.

This Douc Langur family, in residence at the San Diego Zoo, is of the yellow-faced race. Unusual in appearance, it is one of the most fascinating species of primates.

Infant Elephants stay close together for company as they get used to new home at Lion Country Safari.

The tiny face and one little hand of a baby Celebes Crested Macaque are just visible as it clings to mother's underside as mama moves about the compound at the Los Angeles Zoo.

Whether in the nursery building, the children's zoo compound, or elsewhere in a zoo or wildlife preserve, animal parents and their offspring are always attention-getters.

Nadula warns intruders away from her infant cubs as one twin sleeps and the other blissfully nurses. Papa Lion is the famed Frasier of Lion Country Safari.

A foal such as this baby Przewalski Horse is a welcome addition to the San Diego Zoo. Zoos are the last refuge for this species, the last strain of truly wild horses, said to be extinct in their native Mongolia.

Dancer, the National Zoo's baby Reindeer, isn't old enough yet to help Santa with his sleigh.

This newly-born White-bearded Gnu and its mother are part of a herd now roaming the hills of the San Diego Zoo's Wild Animal Park.

Nyandarua, the name given this female baby Bongo, is the first of its species to be born in captivity (August 6, 1971). Officials there consider it to be the most noteworthy birth so far at the National Zoological Park in its conservation and scientific research program. Two pair of this elusive species were brought from their native Africa after considerable field study and effort on the part of Dr. Theodore H. Reed, the Zoo's Director. Accurate records are now being established as to mating and other behavior of these animals.

This Hamadryas Baboon family lives at the San Diego Zoo.

In addition to merely looking at the form of the animal and the so-called antics of some, there are fascinating things to be learned about them. Information about the Hamadryas baboon, for example, reveals that in the wild state it is found in Africa and parts of Yemen and Aden. Long ago in Egypt these creatures were considered to be sacred and drawings of them are still to be seen in temples of that land. It is said by some historians that these intelligent animals were trained to weed gardens, gather fruit, and wait on tables.

Although they spend most of their time on the ground, these baboons can move swiftly along through leafy tree branches. Infants not old enough to get about by themselves hang onto mother and in that way they travel with the troop.

Not only new at the zoo are infant and rare creatures of the animal world, but there are new attitudes, new concepts as to the role which zoos should play in today's world. A good modern zoo is more than an amusement center. Emphasis now is on information and education. There are new and interesting programs for learning about animals and their ways which appeal to people of all ages.

51

The educational centers* of the San Diego Zoo and those in Cincinnati, Milwaukee, and Oklahoma City, for example, are among the finest. Special classes and tours for the handicapped are available at many zoos, such as those for the blind at the Los Angeles Zoo.

At educational centers mysteries of nature are explored; basic facts about plant and animal life are revealed. Through this study of ecology the student learns something of the relationships between plants, animals, and man.

Students may visit the hydroponics room where plants, such as barley, are sprouted without soil. Using water as a growing base, hydroponics units produce green fodder which serves as a health food for captive animals. These are today's magic gardens.

Certain groups will have the thrill of learning about pets, their care, feeding and breeding. They may learn something of animal defenses and how animals have helped man, from the ancient gardening of the Hamadryas baboons to present-day use of elephants for heavy labor in Asia.

Other groups may study bird migrations or make a study of amphibians. In a study of reptiles they may follow with wonder

*The National Zoo, Washington, D. C., also with one of the best of educational centers and which is a pioneer in the field, has for its motto, "Education, Conservation, Recreation and Research."

Baby American Alligator stays close to mother at the Los Angeles Zoo. In the wild, this vanishing species is found only in southern regions of the United States where it spends much of its time dozing in the sun on stream banks or floating under water with just the top of its head visible. A newborn alligator is only about 10 inches long but growth rate is rapid.

the act of a snake shedding its skin. Or they may become acquainted with the great Komodo Dragon, the world's largest lizard. Prehistoric in looks, the "dragon" is native to only three small volcanic islands which lie east of Java in the long chain of Oceanic Islands. A splendid creature, this lizard is a carrion eater but is capable of running down deer, wild boar, and goats.

Keeper Jack De Prato feeds Komodo Dragon at the National Zoo.

*This Arizona Collared Peccary mother and her babies enjoy
a simulated desert environment at the San Diego Zoo.*

The rare Ruffed Lemur is native to the rain forests of north-eastern Madagascar. The babies, unlike most primates, are placed in a nest instead of being carried about by the mother, who returns to the nest periodically to nurse them.

Malaysian Sun Bear.

Young artists are encouraged to express themselves through drawing, sculpture, and photography, with the animals serving as inspiration and live models. One may sketch a snake, another a lamb, or a chimpanzee. Yet another child's interest may be drawn to a collared peccary mother and her babies. There is a whole zooful of animals from which to choose.

This graceful baby Guanaco, native to South America, is related to the llama and the camel.

A young Chimpanzee enjoys watching zoo visitors.

Patrick, the baby Tapir, was born on St. Patrick's Day at the National Zoo.

A baby tapir is a popular subject for the drawing boards of young artists. The tapir is restricted to swampy regions of the Americas and Southern Asia. Mother tapir alone cares for her offspring, whose "watermelon" decorations disappear as it matures.

56

A rare "first" was achieved by the Bronx Zoo when a tufted puffin chick emerged from its burrow where it had hatched some fifty days earlier. It dove into the cold waters of its sea-cliffs home in the Zoo's Aquatic Birds Building to enjoy its first cool swim. A bird of the cold waters of the Northwest Pacific, it became the first member of its species to be bred in captivity anywhere in the world.

Andy Aardvark (above). "Aardvark" is an Afrikaans word meaning "earth pig." Baby Anteater, whose native habitat is South America, waits patiently for small hands to pet him. These two unusual creatures are part of Jett's Petting Zoo which travels about the country.

Choose an animal, any animal from aardvark to zebra, and find out everything you can about the animal of your choice. Spend time watching it at the zoo* and read up on it. If you should choose the aardvark, you will discover that this nocturnal animal is born hairless and helpless. It too cries like a human baby. Hump-backed and rabbit-eared, this strange creature is often called a biological wonder. In the wild it lives on ants and termites which it digs out with sharp claws, catching them up with its long, slim, sticky tongue. The aardvark, native to Africa, digs a burrow which is sometimes taken over by a sly and seldom-seen aardwolf.

*Not all species of animals are exhibited at any one given zoo. Even if it isn't possible to spend much time at the zoo, it's still an exciting adventure to read about the wonders of wildlife.

Buttons, a Pigmy Chimpanzee, does his balancing act in the Children's Zoo in San Diego. About a year-and-a-half old here, he was approximately nine months old when brought to the Zoo from his native Africa.

If you should choose the hippopotamus, you will discover among other things that this "river horse" bears and suckles its young under water. The baby nurses for about a minute, then comes up to breathe, diving down again for another bit of nourishment. Mother takes great care to keep her infant away from its father lest it be crushed by his enormous, heavy body.

Or if you should choose to study the mandrill, with its brilliant red and blue facial markings, you will discover that it is a relative of the Hamadryas baboon and cares for its young in similar fashion.

Should you choose the zebra, you will find that this stunningly-striped member of the horse family sometimes kicks and bites like a mule. Foals at birth are able to get up, nurse, and almost immediately frisk along beside the mother. Zebras are not easily tamed. Cunning as baby zebras are, they are not usually among those in the zoo area where petting young animals is allowed.

In the 1930's there was an English innovation called an animal bank from which children could borrow small creatures such as turtles, white mice, or guinea pigs. From this came the idea that there should be something special for children in the regular zoos. This was developed into the "contact idea" where, under supervision, even young children could pet or handle small wild creatures and domestic animals. The idea spread to other countries and now there are children's zoos within most of the larger zoological gardens and animal parks.

This two-week-old baby Fallow Deer and its mother live in Bambi's Hideaway at Montreal's Garden of Wonders (Jardin des Merveilles).

In Edmonton, Canada, there is the Storyland Valley Zoo where animals of nursery story fame, such as the Three Little Pigs, live in storybook houses. In Montreal there is the Jardin des Merveilles (Garden of Wonders). Infant animals and pets on display in these special children's zoos may range from rabbits, mice, and de-scented skunks, to llamas, lambs, goats, and baby deer. Young "petting" animals are rotated so that they do not receive too much handling without a rest.

Temple of the Sun in the same "little zoo within a zoo," which is part of the Montreal Zoological Park, is home to this ten-day-old baby Llama and its mother.

In the San Diego Children's Zoo, as at any number of others, the "Mouse House" is a specially baked loaf of bread in which mice live. They nibble away at their house to their hearts' content, and climb in and out of window-like holes to scamper about their enclosure. Baby chicks may be seen hatching from eggs kept warm in a poultry incubator. Nearby, baby elephants stretch exploring trunks to the small outstretched hands of human children.

From time to time young creatures are graduated from the nursery into the Children's Zoo. In turn, as they grow older, they are moved from there into the zoo proper or are sent to other zoos where they will be cared for in suitable surroundings.

There are traveling zoos which take animals to schools, hospitals, and to city parks. Through the traveling zoo people of all ages, from tiny toddlers on up to grandparents, may become acquainted with animals brought for display by the "Zooleader" or teacher. Some get up the courage to touch a snake as well as to pet a baby llama or other furry young creature. Chicago's Lincoln Park Zoo has pioneered in this exciting venture.

Children sit enthralled as they listen to talk about animals as the Lincoln Park Traveling Zoo visits a Chicago park.

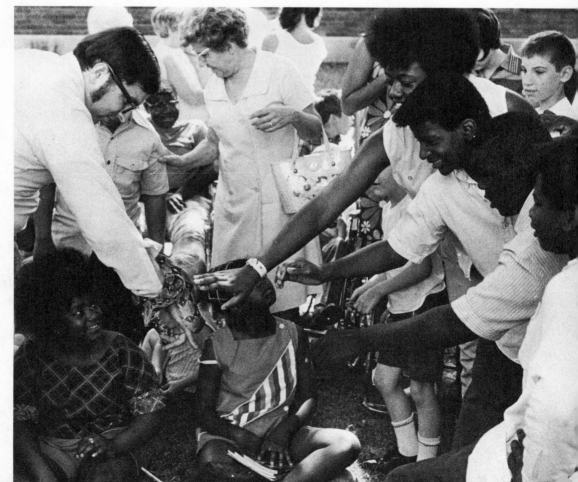

To many city dwellers, children and older people alike, farm animals are as exotic as are lions and tigers, and a model farm is among the newer exhibits at some zoos.

The Lincoln Park Zoo has a fine example of such an attraction. This little farm in the city exhibits beef cattle and other farm animals. Here are to be seen cows with their calves, horses and their foals, mother pigs with their piglets. Hens, ducks, and geese and their fluffy offspring are also part of the farmyard scene.

This remarkable farm, complete with barns, is within view of Chicago's busy traffic and high-rise apartments. The Farm was a gift to "city folks" from the Lincoln Park Zoological Society and the Chicago Park District.

68

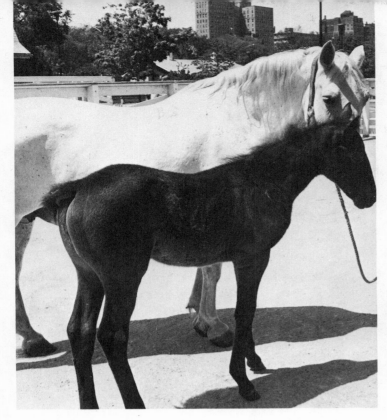

Lippizan mare and colt in outdoor corral at Horse Barn, Chicago's Farm-in-the-Zoo. Lippizan colts are dark gray but turn white as they grow older.

The Farm is but a small part of the Lincoln Park Zoo whose wildlife collection is one of the finest. A veterinarian skilled in caring for farm animals is among those who help to keep this Zoo's animals in tip-top condition.

Little boys are spellbound at their first sight of a baby lamb drinking milk from a bottle held by Farm Animal Keeper.

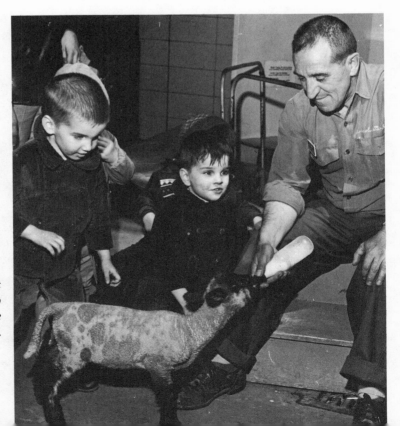

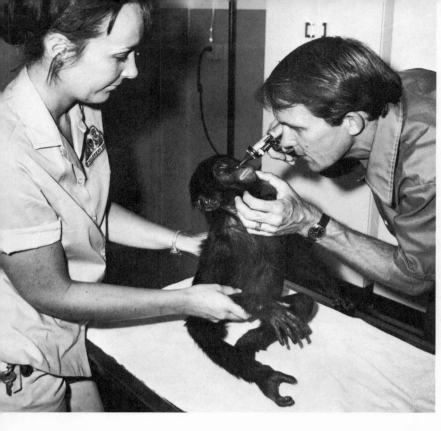

Check-up for a chimp. Pigmy Chimpanzee Lorel is a good hospital patient as Dr. Charles Sedgwick, San Diego Zoo veterinarian, examines her nose. Sue Schroeder, Children's Zoo nursery attendant, gives Lorel moral as well as physical support.

Where there are full-time zoo veterinarians, such as at Lincoln Park, San Diego, and other major zoos, the doctor is always in. He may aid in the delivery of animal babies if the mother needs help. This may take place in the hospital building, out in a paddock or grotto, or other maternity den.

From elephant to baby chick, from tortoise to giraffe, the veterinarian tends to his patients, treating them for whatever ails them. They may be suffering from a severe stomach upset caused by a thoughtless or malicious visitor tossing them inedible objects. The death of many an animal has been caused from swallowing coins, bottle caps, matches, and even unsuitable kinds of food.

This Aldabra Tortoise with a cast on its broken leg has a skateboard to help it get around while leg is mending. It lives at the National Zoo in Washington, D. C.

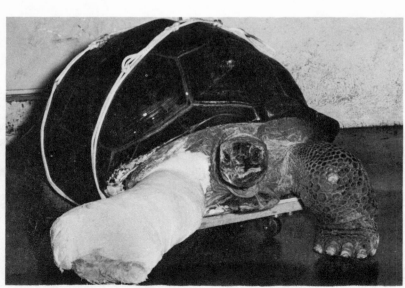

Peter the Cheetah also sports a cast on a broken leg. He is getting ready, somewhat hesitantly, to try it out in the San Diego Zoo hospital.

Animals may be treated for sore feet, a toothache, or even a broken leg. One veterinarian advises that animals often suffer from cuts of one kind or another. Primates, especially, suffer from colds, the flu, and other respiratory diseases. An orangutan, gorilla, or chimpanzee with a runny nose is just as miserable, or more so, than are human beings with a cold. Sometimes it is necessary to put them in isolation in the zoo hospital for their own protection and that of the other animals.

At the same hospital, Dr. William Rapley, a veterinarian intern, and Keeper Murray Malcom examine the wing of an injured Red-tailed Hawk brought in for treatment by the Humane Society. The bird is restrained for examination in a stockinette, a standard procedure for working with such birds.

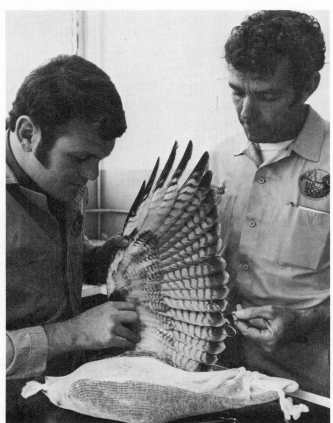

Zoo veterinarians and keepers are sometimes questioned about the birth of a baby giraffe. Does it start life with a short neck, or is it possible that such a creature is born intact with long neck and long legs? It is difficult to imagine such a baby being tucked away in the mother's body, which is quite short and compact even though she may be over fifteen feet tall. But a newborn giraffe is complete with elongated neck,* stilt-like legs, and short little horns. At the moment of birth the hair-and-skin-covered horns, common to both sexes, are down over the forehead. Then in a matter of two or three hours the horns are standing erect.

It was way back in 1889 that the first giraffe to be born in zoo captivity was delivered at the Cincinnati Zoo. This was cause for great rejoicing. Although not uncommon today, the birth of an infant giraffe to a mother in residence at a zoo is still cause for rejoicing.

A newborn giraffe may weigh anywhere from about eighty-five to 125 pounds, sometimes more. It may be five to six feet tall. There have been those unusually large babies who have weighed as much as 175 pounds and measured nearly seven feet in height.

If all goes well at its entry into the world, the infant is soon up on its feet after a few unsuccessful wobbly attempts. Then, with possibly a nudge from mother, it nuzzles up to her and makes fumbling attempts to find the milk supply. This accomplished, the satisfying business of nursing begins. When not suckling her baby the mother spends much time in grooming her child, nipping at its little mane, putting every stiff hair in place with her big soft lips.

Usually in a matter of days, parent animals are reunited after having been separated for a time before the baby's birth.** The young animal then becomes acquainted with its father who takes a hand in teaching it the ways of a giraffe. The baby follows its parents, watching them and imitating their movements. The older ones reach up to browse among the treetops and the young giraffe soon tries to reach up to the leaves.

*Long as it is, a giraffe's neck contains only the usual seven vertebrae common to all mammals, human beings included.

**This applies to many other animals as well, orangutans, gorillas, and bears among them. This precaution is taken to lessen the possibility of injury or death to the newborn infant.

A baby giraffe is weaned at about eight or nine months, at which time it is eating everything its parents do, although it may continue to nurse at night for a time longer. In the zoo the leaf diet is supplemented with hay, fruits and vegetables.

Due to the length of its neck, it is necessary for a giraffe, even a baby, to take a spraddle-legged, awkward-looking stance in order to drink or pick up a twig or leaf from the ground.

Generally thought to be mute, these animals do have vocal cords, although they are somewhat underdeveloped. On occasion they may make small sounds. A mother giraffe has been heard giving a low call when her child strayed too far away. A baby giraffe has been heard bleating softly when it lost sight of its mother.

In the wild, in their native Africa, giraffes live in groups, with an adult male usually leading a number of females and their young. In very remote areas groups are often considerably larger. These herds may include newly-born infants, grandparent animals, aunts, uncles, and young giraffe cousins.

Births are usually single, although a few instances of twin giraffes have been reported. Early in 1972 a giraffe without spots was born in the Ueno Zoological Gardens in Tokyo, Japan, the third such unusual unspotted white giraffe known to be alive at that time.

Albert, The People-Watcher.

Some zoo animals return the interest of their human counterparts and become people-watchers. Albert, the San Diego Zoo's silver-backed gorilla, is one of these. He came to the Zoo from his native Africa as an eight-pound, six-month-old infant. He has made many friends among regular zoo visitors during his long years in residence. Now he teaches the ways of a gorilla to the young of his kind who share his living quarters.

In the wild a mother gorilla guards her baby closely. She carries it around with her as she moves about with the troop, clutching it tightly against her breast with one arm. At three months baby is able to ride on mother's back. At a year a baby gorilla is playing with other youngsters in the troop. They wrestle with each other and practice chest-thumping as they imitate actions of their elders. Father gorilla sometimes plays with the young, allowing them to crawl all over him.

Few gorillas have been born in captivity, although they do well in zoos when brought from their native habitat. Thus excitement ran especially high at the Cincinnati Zoo when two pair of these prized creatures each produced offspring within eight days of each other. Cincinnati's joy was complete when the infants turned out to be a male and a female, Sam and Samantha.

Sam and Samantha.

Once a zoo-goer, child or grownup, gets caught up in making visits to animal friends such as Albert Gorilla, or Sam and Samantha; Ken-Alan Orangutan, Molly Giraffe, or Frieda Polar Bear and her cubs, his life is made the richer.

Once people become caught up in working in a zoo, whether as veterinarian, director, curator, or keeper, they usually stay in the business. Infant animals form one of the strong bonds that keep them in this important work that may require long and anxious hours watching over the creatures under their care. For them the birth of any baby animal is a pleasing event, a welcome addition to the zoo. When a "first-in-captivity" birth takes place it is especially gratifying. News of the infant offspring's arrival is greeted enthusiastically, not only by zoo personnel but by zoological society members and interested people all over the world.

Time was when few indeed were the baby animals of any kind born in a zoo. But the hard-won knowledge gained through painstaking study of animal diets, breeding patterns, and behavior is beginning to show results. In increasing numbers zoo-kept creatures, rare as well as those more common, are mating and giving birth to infant offspring. Rare and endangered species may yet be saved and man will have the pleasure of their company.

It's an exciting adventure to go to the zoo, whether to seek out a favorite animal or to visit all its residents with equal interest. And with indoor and outdoor nurseries beginning to bulge with appealing babies of all shapes and sizes, it's a delight to discover that there's always something new at the zoo.

Animals procreate, each after its own kind. Here, Frasier with his lionesses and cubs form a contented family group (pride) in their simulated natural habitat at Lion Country Safari (California).

INDEX

PICTURE CREDITS

Australian News and Information Bureau
  20, 22, 25, 77 (top left), Back jacket; 2, 24 (W. Brindle); 23, 29 (top) (Michael Brown); 21, 27 (H. Frauca); 28, 29 (bottom), 31 (Neil Murray); 30 (W. Pederson)

Cincinnati Zoo
  75 (bottom) (Julianne Warren)

Jardin des Merveilles
  63

Lincoln Park Zoo
  66, 67, 68, 69

Lion Country Safari
  8, 33, 49 (bottom), 76

New York Zoological Society (The Bronx Zoo)
  57

Oklahoma City Zoo
  11 (top)

San Diego Zoo
  Front jacket, 10, 13, 15, 16, 17, 18, 19, 37, 38, 44, 48, 50 (top left, center left), 51, 54, 60, 61, 70 (top), 71, 73 (top) (Ron Garrison); 70 (top) (F. D. Schmidt)

Smithsonian Institution (National Zoological Park) 26 (top), 47, 50 (center right, bottom right), 53 (bottom), 56, 70 (bottom)

U.S. Bureau of Sport Fisheries and Wildlife 14, 12 (top) (Ray Erickson); 9 (Luther C. Goldman); 11 (bottom left) (V. B. Scheffer); 12 (bottom) (Rex Schmidt)

Zoological Society of London (England)
  46

All other pictures by Terry Shannon and Charles Payzant, taken at Lion Country Safari, Los Angeles Zoo, San Diego Zoo, and Jett's Petting Zoo